C000056122

THE AUTHORITY GUIDE TO
PR FOR SMALL
BUSINESSES

Use the power of public relations and the media to
reach your target customer and grow your business

STEVE BUSTIN

The Authority Guide to PR for Small Businesses

Use the power of public relations and the media to reach your target customer and grow your business

© Steve Bustin

ISBN 978-1-909116-86-3

eISBN 978-1-909116-87-0

Published in 2017 by Authority Guides

authorityguides.co.uk

The right of Steve Bustin to be identified as the author of this work has been asserted by him in accordance with the Copyright, Designs and Patents Act 1988.

A CIP record of this book is available from the British Library.

All rights reserved. No part of this book may be reproduced, stored in a retrieval system, or transmitted in any form or by any means, electronic, mechanical, photocopying, recording or otherwise, without the prior written permission of the publisher.

No responsibility for loss occasioned to any person acting or refraining from action as a result of any material in this publication can be accepted by the author or publisher.

Printed in the United Kingdom.

Acknowledgements

This book would not have been possible without the help and input from a wide range of people, including:

- Sue, Kelly, Chris, Bella, Maria and the team at SRA Books.

- The journalists who agreed to be interviewed and to share their advice: Guy Clapperton, Chris Johnston, Alice Hart-Davis, Peter Lindsay and Sarah Fountain.

- The journalists who kindly contributed their top tips: Sarah Lewis, Scott Solder, Rachael Glazier, Michael Dodd, Pattie Barron, Penny Haslam, Gary Duffy and Rob Ashton.

- The businesses who agreed to act as case studies and let me write about their PR successes.

- Photographer James MacDonald of Silver Fox Imaging for the back cover portrait.

- My husband John Williams for proofreading, providing support and making endless cups of tea. I really couldn't have done it without him.

For regional press ensure you say where you live or where you're from. I get fed up with businesses and PRs saying they're local and then discovering they're from out of the area we cover.

**Sarah Lewis
journalist**

Contents

Nothing beats a compelling top line, an interesting bit of data, a new trend or an engaging human interest story. Make sure you have the best possible spokesperson to tell the story and that they are available and flexible and if you can, it helps to supply images or multi-media to whet the appetite of a lazy or hard-pressed newsroom.

Gary Duffy
journalist

Introduction

Have you ever wondered why your local newspaper always writes about your competitor but not you? Or why the trade magazine for your industry sector calls on other people to give expert comment rather than you? Or why the BBC News website never seems to feature organisations like yours?

The people, businesses and organisations who *do* get featured in the media are normally those that are undertaking some public relations (PR).

If you want to be covered by the media, from a local paper to national TV, you have to put yourself out there, letting journalists know who you are and what you're doing. You have to be proactive, imaginative, tenacious and committed. The results, however, can be extraordinary. One piece of media coverage in the right outlet, reaching the right audience with the right message can be the making of your business. All with remarkably little work and zero budget.

I'm a big believer in the power of PR and the media to transform a business from little-known bit player to a high-profile (even if still small) business punching well above its weight and reaching out to potentially huge audiences.

Case study

Owen Reading runs Eyejusters (eyejusters.com), an Oxford-based company making glasses with adjustable focus. Owen attended a PR course I ran a few years ago and using the press release he wrote on the course, started getting coverage – and seeing results – very quickly.

Our press release got us a small paragraph in the Mail on Sunday *at the bottom of the health notes column. The interest that generated on our website was enough to clear our warehouse as we made a month's worth of sales in a single day. The publication was spot on for our target audience but I was still amazed something that small could get such impressive results.*

Since then we've had another piece in the Mail on Sunday, *this time getting a half page including some lovely images. We did six months' worth of sales in a day.*

There's no doubt that the right story put in front of the right people can generate so much more than an advert would have generated. One of the important things for our company is that people trust us as an unknown brand with a different type of product. People trust what they read in the newspaper. It's an incredibly cost-effective way of getting your name out there.

How I learned about the power of PR for business

I've spent much of my career on one side or the other of the 'divide' between PR and the media. I started my career working as a researcher then broadcast journalist for BBC News, first in radio and then in TV. For a couple of years I worked on the Newsgathering planning desk, part of the team that plans for forthcoming news stories (and you'd be amazed how much 'news' can actually be planned in advance). This desk is also the 'intake' point for many of the press releases sent to the BBC newsroom, so I regularly had to sit down with a pile of hundreds of press releases and sift through them. You very quickly learn how to spot a good story – and how to discard the vast majority of releases with only a glance. I learned what makes an eye-catching story and how best to communicate it.

When I moved into PR, first working for a lifestyle 'dot-com' then running my own PR agency, that ability to know instinctively what was or wasn't a story stood me in good stead, as did understanding the pressures a journalist works under. Alongside my PR career I've continued to write as a freelance print journalist for national newspapers and magazines, most recently for gardening magazines (although I've always kept my PR and journalism work completely separate so, no, I never wrote about my clients).

Being an active journalist means that I still receive press releases daily and it never ceases to amaze me quite how bad many of them are, with no story, no topicality or no relevance to the publications I write for. It's tempting to email back to the PR professional or business who has sent the release with a critique and an explanation of why they haven't got a chance of getting coverage, but thus far I've restrained myself. Maybe I should just send them a copy of this book?

What has become clear is that while a PR consultant or agency may have the contacts and industry knowledge, no one can 'sell' your business like you can. I'm certainly not saying you shouldn't work with a PR professional (I wouldn't have made a living from it for so many years if people didn't) but many small businesses, charities and community groups simply don't have the budget to do so. Getting media coverage by undertaking PR is absolutely within the reach of any small organisation. As a small business owner myself, I've see the power of what even relatively small pieces of media coverage can do to sales and the bottom line.

How to use this book

This book outlines a process that if followed from start to finish will guide you through the stages needed to run a successful PR campaign. I suggest you start by reading it from beginning to end, so you understand all the elements you'll need to put in place. Then return to page 1 and start putting it all into practice, doing the exercises and absorbing the top tips.

If you have some PR experience or once you've run your first campaign, the book is also designed to be a reference guide, something to dip back into when you need ideas or inspiration for your next set of PR activity. If you're wondering whether your story idea is newsworthy or looking for some thoughts on how to generate media coverage when you don't have a current story, there's a chapter to refer to. If you're wondering what else you could do to boost the coverage you're getting, turn to the relevant chapter and refresh your PR campaign.

A few words about language

The media is a broad church including national newspapers, local papers, consumer magazines, trade and specialist magazines, national and local radio and TV and online media outlets. Between them, these outlets have readers, users, listeners and viewers.

For ease, throughout this book when I refer to 'the media' you should take that to encompass any print, broadcast and online media, unless I single out a specific tool or tactic as being appropriate to only one form of media. When I refer to 'the audience' I mean readers, listeners and/or viewers.

Likewise in business, I might mention your 'product' or 'service' as a catchall for whatever you sell to generate revenue. If you're a charity or other type of organisation you may not see yourself as 'selling' anything, but don't let that put you off as the approach I'm about to outline will work just as well for you, too.

Finally I consider 'PR' and 'public relations' to be interchangeable so I'm going to use both liberally. So let's dive in to what this actually means.

Offer a free regular column on whatever
you do to your local website – which is
probably desperate for content.

Scott Solder
journalist

What is PR and what can it do for your business?

So what is PR?

The Chartered Institute of Public Relations (cipr.co.uk) defines it as:

Public Relations is about reputation – the result of what you do, what you say and what others say about you.

Public Relations is the discipline which looks after reputation, with the aim of earning understanding and support and influencing opinion and behaviour. It is the planned and sustained effort to establish and maintain goodwill and mutual understanding between an organisation and its publics.

Let's just unpick that a little. Reputation is key to any business. Before people can form an opinion of you or your product, they have to have heard of you. You may be creating the best product in the world but if you're not out talking about it in public, no one is going to buy it.

Do you really need to influence opinion and behaviour? Absolutely. If you're a business, a charity, a community group or any other organisation, you won't exist for long if you're not able to influence the opinion and behaviour of those you seek to serve or sell to. You need them to change their purchasing behaviour in your favour. You need them to think positively about you in order to buy from you again or talk about you to friends.

Finally, note the plural use of the word 'publics'. You may well have several different audiences. You may need to communicate with existing customers, prospects, suppliers, whole new market sectors and even with policymakers and politicians. Each audience may need a different message via a different channel. You won't reach them if the message or channel is wrong.

If, for example, you're trying to reach urban young people as customers but you're seeking coverage in *The Daily Telegraph* (because that's what you read yourself), you will not get the results you require as your target audience won't see it as it's the wrong media channel. You have to find your audiences and reach out to them via *their* channels and in *their* language. Much more to come on this throughout this book.

Public relations, especially as provided by PR agencies, covers the gamut of services, from the 'Absolutely Fabulous' champagne-swilling world of celebrity parties and product placement to the 'Malcolm Tucker' beer-swilling (or should that be cappuccino swilling) world of political spin and Machiavellian scheming to steer and 'manage' the news agenda. Throw in services such as reputation management and crisis communications and it can feel that PR is too specialist a skill set for most small businesses or entrepreneurs.

But (and it's a big but) all these PR services have the same aim: building awareness of a particular entity or message and the management of how it is perceived.

For most small businesses, the focus of their PR activity is securing editorial media coverage in newspapers and magazines, on radio or TV or online. That's what this book will teach you to do. I'm going to explain the process you need to follow to reach out to the *right* media for your business to reach the *right* audience with the *right* message at the *right* time. While reputation management, crisis communications and all the other facets of PR are important, they're beyond the scope of this book (although many of the techniques I'm going to look at will help with those aspects). For most businesses, PR is about wanting to see their name in the papers to reach their target audience and thus make more money.

Why should your business undertake PR?

I firmly believe every small business would be foolish to miss out on the opportunity to secure media coverage through PR, for four main reasons:

- Media coverage gives you the opportunity to connect to both a huge audience and a precisely targeted audience.

  If you're launching a consumer product, you want to get that product in front of as many of your potential customers as possible. As Owen found in the case study in the introduction to this book, even a small piece of coverage in a national newspaper can trigger huge volumes of sales.

  Many of the small business owners I coach on PR express doubts about their ability to secure national media coverage, but a good product is a good product, regardless of the size of the company behind it. Your product or business is just as deserving of national media coverage as anyone else's.

Sometimes, however, it's not the size of the audience that matters but the targeted nature of that audience. Niche media outlets allow you to directly reach really specific audiences.

If you were launching or promoting a service aimed solely at gardeners, for example, you could reach those people by targeting the media outlets they consume. If you were promoting a business-to-business (B2B) product or service, you could target your exact customers using their sector's trade magazines, websites, blogs and so on.

- Getting media coverage is a fantastic way to build credibility. Being able to say 'As seen on TV' or 'Click here to read about us in the press' on your website or social media pages is an immediate qualifier. It says 'We're being talked about, we're noteworthy' to customers and potential customers who may be checking you out.

If a customer is looking to buy a product or service, they may well look for third-party recommendations and testimonials, and what better testimonial is there than coverage in a publication or media outlet they trust?

- Gaining media coverage can be great for your search engine optimisation (SEO). Most print publications now reproduce their content online (even if it's behind a paywall) and any links to or mentions of your website (or even just business name) can really help to boost you up search rankings, especially if the coverage is from a major media outlet such as the BBC or a national newspaper.

Media coverage also makes *great* social media and blog content that you (and hopefully your customers) can share across multiple platforms, extending its reach and impact.

- Securing media coverage can give an enormous morale boost within your business. Everyone wants to feel that they're working for a company that is respected and being talked about (for the right reasons) or that the product or service they're working on is being reviewed in very positive terms.

Being able to pin up print media coverage on the wall or share broadcast coverage online with your team can have the most amazing effect on staff loyalty and productivity. It can also help you to attract the best candidates when you're recruiting, as people want to work for a company or on a product that's being talked about.

Media coverage and profile is also often used as part of the measure of the value of a company when it's being sold.

What can PR do for your business?

PR can achieve a range of goals for your business. The main target is usually going to be sales: selling more products or services as a result of putting your message in front of your target audience. Alternatively, the goals of a PR campaign could be around driving traffic to a website, selling tickets for an event, driving footfall to a shop, publicising the appointment of new senior staff or signing a big new client or deal. It might also be about raising the personal profile of the business owner, establishing them as a voice of authority or spokesperson for their industry.

Just like any other marketing activity, you should go into a PR campaign with clear goals or objectives. If you haven't set goals, how are you going to know whether your campaign is working or not?

Top tip

Don't just launch into your PR activity with a vague notion of wanting to raise awareness or being better known. Be strategic. Who do you want to reach and what do you want them to do as a result of hearing about your business?

Exercise

Write down three things you'd like PR to achieve for your business.

What would be a good measure of success for you and your PR campaign?

Working with a journalist: Chris Johnson

Chris is a former business news editor for *The Times* and now writes business stories for *The Guardian* and BBC News Online.

It's unusual for national newspapers to cover a small business's story, although some now have Enterprise correspondents or editors who look specifically at stories relevant to SMEs [small and medium-sized enterprises], so seek them out.

The problem is that news editors don't care that a tiny company has opened a new store or appointed a new senior vice president. If your product or service really makes a difference for customers, however, and is truly innovative, it may work as a story for a national paper. Find something compelling about your business or product. Always try to have a human angle, too, whether that's about the chief executive or the customer. Having no human voice makes a story very dull.

We still need to see a press release, too. It makes it easier for us to quickly see what the story is and what's going on. The less hyperbole the better, though.

Another way you can approach a national newspaper is by positioning yourself as an expert commentator rather than sending a press release or story in.

Read the publication first to make sure your business is relevant to its readers. Also, by reading the magazine/newspaper/website, it'll allow you to tailor your pitch to that publication or a specific section of that publication.

Rachael Glazier
journalist

What's so special about editorial coverage?

The holy grail of most business PR activity is editorial coverage in your target media outlets.

Editorial is the content or copy produced by journalists. It's news stories, features and reports. It's also the editorial photos, videos and audio clips. The journalist has chosen to cover this story – no one has paid them to do so or to influence the tone of their coverage. Whether it's a news story in a newspaper, a feature in a magazine, a report on radio or an appearance on TV – or their online equivalents – it's what your PR activity should be aiming for.

Put simply, editorial coverage is content written by journalists that isn't advertising, so hasn't been paid for.

Is editorial really any better than advertising?

Think about what you do when you read a newspaper or flick through a magazine. Do your eyes get drawn to the stories and features or the adverts? We've become incredibly good at filtering out adverts, especially in print media, despite the best efforts of the advertising industry to make their ads eye-catching and engaging. If we *do* look at an advert, do we trust it and treat its content in the same way as a piece of editorial?

Editorial is more likely to be read, believed and trusted, and more likely to be acted upon. The reason is that editorial contains an implicit third-party endorsement of whatever is being covered. The journalist has made a decision that this 'thing' (be it a topic, issue, product, service or business) is worth them writing about – and thus worth you reading about.

We trust media outlets to have sifted out the stories that aren't worth reading and to only present us with the stories that are worthy of our attention. The journalist is basically saying, 'In my expert opinion, this story is worth you knowing about and will be interesting and relevant to you.'

An advert, on the other hand, is simply something that someone has paid for – they've said what they want presented, where it should appear, when and how often. It's not independent and it certainly doesn't contain the implicit endorsement of a piece of editorial.

What about advertorial?

When coaching businesses on PR skills, I'm often asked whether it wouldn't be easier to buy an advertorial in their magazine of choice. You pay your money and you get final say over what it includes. Surely that's a safer option as you're guaranteed to get your key message across?

Well yes, that *might* get your key message across, but when was the last time you read something with the words 'advertorial', 'advertising feature' or 'promotion' written above it? An advertorial is an advert dressed up to look like editorial, but most of us filter them out as we know they're going to be partisan and self-aggrandising rather than balanced and fair.

Personally, I think buying an advertorial is a waste of money as it lacks that third-party endorsement and has a whiff of trying to 'cheat' the readers into believing it's editorial.

A few words about 'online PR' and SEO

Does online content count as editorial? As a general rule, if it's written by a journalist, then yes. Every media outlet has an online equivalent. Many, such as *The Guardian* or *Daily Mail* websites, produce far more content online than appears in the print version. A piece of editorial coverage on a big name website can deliver fantastic results for your business. *Daily Mail Online*, for example, has an incredibly responsive readership and I've seen some small business websites crash under the unexpected spike of traffic after coverage has appeared there. Online outlets should certainly be on your list of target media.

A few years ago a number of companies started to advertise 'online PR' services. They weren't PR providers, however, but SEO (Search Engine Optimisation) consultancies, promising to get clients online coverage and links, purely to boost their search engine rankings. The problem was that all they were doing was taking a 'press release' or a piece of copy and getting it uploaded on as many websites as possible. It was purely a numbers game: it didn't matter whether anyone read it, let alone whether it was worth reading about, just that search engines could find it. This *isn't* PR.

Working with a journalist: Sarah Fountain

Sarah Fountain is the planning editor in the BBC News Business Unit, producing business stories for all BBC News radio and TV outlets.

The main opportunity for small businesses to get coverage on BBC Radio and TV news is as a case study. We're always looking for small business owners with opinions and who are willing to talk. For example, every month we cover the latest employment figures or interest rates and we need to illustrate those stories and the effects the new figures have on small businesses.

We often struggle to find businesses who are happy to talk, especially about struggles they may be facing, but the im-pact of your business appearing on the Six O'Clock News *can be huge.*

We're not looking to publicise your product or business but can use you to help tell the story. For instance, tomorrow we're running a story about how rural businesses need to diversify to survive so I'm looking for a small rural business who has done just that.

When I'm looking for a business to use as a case study I'll go to local Chambers of Commerce, industry associations, lo-cal councils or the Federation for Small Businesses, so make sure those types of organisations know you're happy to talk to the media.

Business stories are often actually people stories, espe-cially for BBC Breakfast *or* Radio 5 Live*. It's definitely worth* *putting yourself forward if you've got a viewpoint or exempli-fy a wider story such as businesses that have been flooded.*

Do send us a press release and while we may not cover your story, we do clock those businesses that we can call on next time we need a case study or that type of story. The best email address to send to is bizplan@bbc.co.uk

Set yourself up as an expert commentator on whatever your business offers – by introducing yourself to local papers/radio/TV/websites. Local expertise is very attractive to local media.

Scott Solder
journalist

Finding your news stories

The first thing you need to decide when starting your PR campaign is what you're going to talk about to the media. A journalist won't just write about you because you ask them to. They'll want to know *why* they should write about you and why *now*. They'll want to know what the story is, and it's up to you to provide them with a suitable story. Don't expect them to find it for you.

Top tip

To secure editorial coverage you need to develop a story for a journalist to cover.

For most small businesses undertaking PR, the easiest type of story to find is a news story.

What is a news story?

What is news? News is, at its most basic level, what's new. Newspapers are the papers that tell us what's new. News broadcasts tell us the new(s) stories, the new developments, the new events.

News is also what people are interested in knowing about. Something can be new but of no interest. People are interested in things that are relevant to them and their lives or their view of the wider world.

The starting point for developing a news story is to think about what's new – and interesting – in your business.

What's new in your business?

Exercise

Make a list of as many things you can think of that might be new in your business over the next year or two.

This list will vary according to the nature of your business and where you are in the business cycle (from start-up to established business) but might include:

- New business (the launch of your business may well be the biggest news story you ever have as you are, by definition, new)
- New product
- New service
- New event
- New premises/shop
- New senior staff appointment
- New job opportunities
- New sponsorship deal
- New charitable activity
- New award or prize
- New major client signing
- New figures or financial results

- New research findings
- New website (although new websites are rarely newsworthy these days unless they've got some functionality that's never been seen before)

Keep you list 'active', adding additional new things as they occur to you, for future story ideas.

Is your story newsworthy? Does it pass the 'So what?' test?

Just because something is new in your business, that doesn't necessarily make it newsworthy. To be newsworthy, it has to be new but it also has to be *interesting*.

Exercise

Select one new thing that you might choose to promote through PR from the previous exercise. Examine that idea critically. Who might this story be interesting or relevant to? If you told your mates in the pub about this news story, would they be interested?

If you told your colleagues, peers or fellow businesspeople about the story, would they be more interested? Or would they say, 'So what?', too?

If your mates wouldn't be interested then chances are it's not a story for a newspaper or magazine read by people like them. If your business contacts *are* interested, however, then it may well be a good story for a business or trade magazine or the business pages of a newspaper or website.

This 'So what?' test is important, as a journalist will apply exactly the same test, putting themselves in the shoes of their readers, viewers or listeners. Would that audience be interested or would they also think, 'So what?' If it's the latter, the journalist won't cover it. If your story passes the 'So what?' test, it's one step closer to being published.

Exercise

Think of a news story about your business that you'd like to release to the media, possibly one from your 'what's new' list. Does it pass the 'So what?' test?

Is your story newsworthy? Does it pass the 'TRUTH' test?

There's a widely used way of checking whether a story is genuinely newsworthy, used by both those in PR and also by journalists considering your story. When I worked on the News Planning desk for BBC News, we would consider hundreds of press releases and story ideas every day and these criteria are the ones each story had to pass.

The TRUTH test isn't about making sure your story is true (although please *always* stick to the truth in a press release, as if a journalist thinks there are lies or exaggerations in there, they'll drop it like a hot stone). Truth is an acronym for what makes a story newsworthy.

T = Topicality

Your story has to be topical or current. News is about what is happening now or has just happened. Think about when you read a newspaper or listen to a bulletin. The stories you read or hear are about what has taken place in the very recent past or are taking place right now.

News only remains newsworthy for a short period of time. I see too many businesses who miss their 'window of topicality' because they think the PR can wait until they're less busy. When you launch your business, you're more likely to be newsworthy because you're new. Once you've been around a few months, you're seen as less fresh, and it may well be that other businesses have launched since who will seem more topical.

Another common mistake I see businesses make regularly is to only send out a press release after an event, when it's no longer topical. Send your release beforehand, not afterwards. Better to be too soon than too late.

Think about how you're going to signal the topicality of your story to the journalist. Why should a journalist write about you today, or for this week's issue? Could it wait until next week's issue, or should it really have been in last week's issue (in which case you've missed the boat)?

Here are four simple ways to signal topicality:

- On your press release, have a 'diary date' at the top rather than today's date. That signals that this is a story for a future date, when it will be topical. This allows a journalist to plan it in for possible future coverage. That diary date will be the date of the event in question, the announcement or the launch.

- In your email subject line, headline and first paragraph, use clear phrases such as 'launching tomorrow', 'released today' or 'to be announced next Monday'. If you find yourself using something along the lines of 'released last week', you're too late.

- Look for a topical news hook. You can give a story a sense of topicality by associating it with something that is topical or in the news, known as a news hook. Really obvious news hooks would be calendar dates such as Valentine's Day, Mother's Day or Halloween. Your news hook could also be something that happens at a specific time of year like the first day of the school term, the Grand National or a local event or anniversary. It could also be a national news story such as the Budget (a lot of businesses release stories 'hooked' on the Budget) or a piece of legislation being introduced or even a cultural event like the opening of a major exhibition or the final of a popular TV show.

Your story does have to have a very obvious relevance to the news hook. 'As schools go back this week, new survey reveals local businesses struggle with staff leaving early to collect their children' would give those survey results topicality.

Keep an eye out for awareness days/weeks/months for possible news hooks. Anything from Comic Relief Day to Be Nice to Nettles Week (yes, honestly, have a look at nettles.org.uk if you don't believe me, it's in May) can provide a good hook for your story.

- Celebrate a business birthday or anniversary. Hold a party to celebrate 5, 10 or 50 years in business. Mark the anniversary of an important milestone with a new announcement. Work out when your business hits an important date and put it in your diary now so you can plan accordingly.

Topicality is vital. You'd be amazed at how many press releases I receive that don't even have a date on them, so I've got no idea when this story is meant for – today, tomorrow, next month? I don't have the time to find out and so just delete it and move on to a story that *is* clearly topical.

Exercise

Look at a story you're considering sending to the press. Is it topical? If not yet, when will it be topical?

R = Relevance

A story can be relevant to a journalist or media outlet in one of two ways.

- Geographical relevance

  Local and regional newspapers, radio stations, magazines and TV stations will almost certainly have a map on their newsroom wall. On that map will be a clear red line covering the boundary of the geographical area that they cover. If you and/or your story are inside that red line you are relevant to that media outlet, but if you are situated outside that red line then you are not relevant and will struggle to convince them to give you coverage.

  So if you are based in, say, Brighton, you might want to get coverage for your new shop in the local press, so you would probably contact *The Argus*, Juice FM and possibly Latest TV. If, however, you contact the *Worthing Herald* or the *Eastbourne Herald* (the neighbouring local papers) about a shop in Brighton, both newspapers are likely to tell you that you're not relevant to their readership.

  Sometimes you can make yourself more relevant to a geographically specific media outlet, however. Using the Brighton example, if you were able to tell the *Worthing Herald* that you'd grown up in Worthing, still lived in the town and were now taking everything you'd learned about business in Worthing but applying it to the neighbouring town, the *Worthing Herald* might now be more interested, because there's a local angle for them. If you want to raise your profile in a new geographical area, think about how you are going to make your story relevant to that area.

- Topical relevance

  While some media outlets cover very specific geographical areas, others cover very specific topic areas. From *Gardeners' World* on BBC2 or *Dogs Monthly* magazine to *Marketing Week* or *Law in Action* on Radio 4, these outlets know their topics and know their audience. They know they have to keep all their content relevant to that audience.

  For example, if you are launching a new B2B service and you've identified lawyers and solicitors as a target market, you need to identify the media outlets for whom your story may be relevant. Send it to radio programme *Law in Action* and online news site *Legal Week* and your story is likely to be seen as relevant to both the journalist and their readers or listeners, so stands a higher chance of gaining coverage (as long as it's not too commercial or an advert masquerading as a story). Send it to *Accountancy Age* magazine, however, and they're going to take one look and think, 'That's about lawyers, not accountants, so it's not relevant' and hit the delete button pretty quickly.

  So your story (and subsequent press release) must be relevant to the media outlet's area of specialism. You can, of course, make your story relevant to them by tweaking it as needed, for example rewriting your press release to highlight how this new service is perfect for accountants and sending that to *Accountancy Age* rather than the legal version.

  It's also worth bearing in mind that on many publications, different journalists will have different specialisms, so your story may only be relevant to certain people on the team. It's worth finding the right specialist to ensure relevance. More about finding the right person to send your story to in a later chapter.

Exercise

Looking at the story you were working on above, is it relevant? Does it have geographical or topical relevance?

U = Unusual

There's an old adage among journalists that 'dog bites man' isn't a story but that 'man bites dog' is definitely a story. 'Man bites dog' is a story because it's unusual, it's not what you expect to read, whereas a dog biting a man is much more common and happens regularly, so isn't newsworthy.

Journalists are always on the lookout for something different, something unusual, something that will make their audience want more. This ties in to the 'So what?' test.

To stand more chance of being newsworthy, your story needs to stand out as being unusual. It may be unusual because it is about something genuinely new that people won't have heard of before. It may be unusual because it turns a common story or assumption on its head. It may be unusual because it makes people gasp, say 'Wow' or even 'Oh no.' It may be unusual because it's humorous or throws new light on an old topic.

If your story is predictable, run-of-the-mill or 'same old, same old' then it's unlikely to be covered. What makes your story stand out from the crowd? What makes it different? What makes it unique?

Exercise

Is your story unusual in some way? What makes it different?

T = Trouble

Like it or not, disagreements, arguments, rows and a bit of controversy make a great story. When was the last time you read about everyone on your local council agreeing? Or about two competing businesses working together in harmony towards common goals? Or an industry spokesperson saying how unbothered they are that the government legislation going through Parliament will make it much harder for businesses to thrive?

If your story is likely to stir things up a little or raise eyebrows, it's more likely to be newsworthy. 'Local business owner says council policy will damage business' is a better news story than 'Local business expert considers other ways council could work with businesses', which is much more passive.

One word of warning. You do need to be prepared to put your head above the parapet on this one. You need to be prepared for people to argue back, to criticise you. This can be a great way to position yourself as a game changer, an industry leader or even a maverick. Do your customers, clients or staff, however, want to think of you as someone who is happy to disrupt the market or would they rather work with a safe pair of hands, a peacemaker? Just something to think about.

Exercise

Is your story controversial in some way or is it likely to stir up trouble of some sort?

H = Human interest

Human interest is now vital to any story, whether it's about consumers and individuals or about large corporates or even world affairs. This is because we are more likely to read a story we can identify with in some way, and we're more likely to identify with another human being than with a corporation. When we consume any media, even trade press, we do so as a person, not as a job title. How will this affect *me*? The journalist will write their coverage aimed at that individual.

So consider how your story affects or impacts the individual. What difference will it make to their lives? How will it make someone's life better, easier, in the workplace or at home? Why do they need your product in their lives? Make the answer to these questions clear in your press release.

A classic way to play up the human interest in your story is by using a case study or testimonial, ideally both. Let us hear about how your product, service, announcement and so on really has made a difference to someone, whether at home or work. Tell us their story, highlighting the problem they had that your product or service helped to solve. Let us hear direct from that person in a first-person testimonial or quote. Let us see them in a picture. That way we're far more likely to identify with them and thus with the benefit your business could bring to us, your potential customers.

We're even more likely to identify with them if they are somehow similar to us. A good way to add relevance to your story as well as human interest is to ensure you have a case study that reflects the audience of the media outlet you're targeting. If you're pitching a story to *Legal Week*, have a case study who is a lawyer. If you're pitching to *Cosmopolitan*, have a case study who is a female aged under 25 (that is, someone who reflects their target readers).

Exercise

Does your story have some element of human interest to the audience you're hoping to reach?

So does your story pass the TRUTH test?

For a story to be newsworthy, it *must* have the first two elements in TRUTH. It must be topical and it must be relevant to the media outlet and their audience. If it's not, it's not newsworthy and is highly unlikely to get coverage.

Ideally, your story will have both topicality and relevance and *at least one* of the other elements: it's unusual, causes trouble or has human interest. If you have a story that has four of these elements, you've got a great story on your hands. If you've got a story that has all five, journalists will be biting your hands off for it.

Exercise

Does your story have topicality *and* relevance *and* at least one of the other three elements of the TRUTH test?

What if there's nothing new in your business?

You're not always going to have something new going on in your business. Sometimes we go through periods of consolidation when we're just doing what we do to make money and don't have anything brand new to make an obvious news story. Yet we still want to undertake PR activity and gain media coverage to keep connecting with existing and potential customers.

Here are three ideas for ways to generate a news story when there's nothing new (or newsworthy) on the horizon.

Create something new

By this I don't mean that you need to create a whole new product or service, but it is perfectly possible to generate something new within your business that will give you something to promote to the media.

New research, results or statistics

This is an absolutely classic way to generate a news story. How often have you heard or read a news story that starts with a sentence like, 'New figures out today suggest that…' or 'New survey has found evidence that…'? New figures often illuminate an issue or give gravitas to an argument so can make a great story as they are both topical (brand new on the day you release them) and relevant to a particular sector or audience. They may well also cause a certain amount of trouble and can be used to underline the human interest in a story.

Create a story by undertaking a new piece of quantitative research or a survey (surveymonkey.com is your friend here) to generate some new statistics or figures that are pertinent to your business or industry.

Two important caveats. First, you need a strong sample size for the figures to be considered robust and meaningful. For a local newspaper your sample size could be 50–100 but for a national newspaper or a trade publication, you really need a sample size of 500+ and ideally over a thousand.

Use social media and your email newsletter list to promote the survey. If necessary incentivise it, offering something in return for taking part, possibly entry into a prize draw for the latest must-have tech gadget or access to the detailed findings when they're available.

You need to be prepared for your figures to be scrutinised and you should make some of the raw data available to journalists, to prove the research is genuine.

The second caveat is that the research or survey needs to say something genuinely new and interesting. Too many businesses undertake a piece of research with an idea of what they'd like the findings to be, so the questions are skewed a certain way. The results of these types of surveys tend to be bland and unexciting, leading people to read the results and think, 'You would say that, wouldn't you?'

Set out to generate research findings that are genuinely exciting, unexpected. Research something that is likely to be of interest to your business sector or to the wider public rather than something only of interest to you.

Exercise

List three questions, survey topics or pieces of research you could undertake to generate new statistics or findings.

Example

Sometimes newsworthy statistics can come about as a by-product of other work. Several years ago I was undertaking a business qualification and as part of my studies I had to undertake some market research. I ran a survey of freelance workers looking at the best business development methods for sole traders and those working freelance, as I was at the time. I sent the survey to everyone I could think of who fitted the bill and asked them to pass it on to others. In the end I had 124 responses.

I was surprised by the results as they showed that 94 per cent of respondents said that the best source of new work wasn't advertising, cold-calling or even networking, but simply asking existing clients to refer them on to others. Perhaps I was naive as I was still relatively new to business at the time, but it hadn't occurred to me simply to ask existing clients for business.

As I was writing up my report, it occurred to me that if this were news to me, it would probably be news to others, too. I wrote the results into a press release and sent it out to all the relevant magazines, websites and outlets focused on small businesses and start-ups. The following week I had coverage in the small business supplement of *The Guardian* (now sadly long gone), on startups.co.uk, Microsoft's SME portal (also now gone) and a number of other websites. I also rewrote the press release to highlight the fact that at the time I was a PR freelancer, and got a nice piece in *PR Week* magazine too.

Those figures had longevity. Over the subsequent three or four years I had a number of requests from other journalists, authors, business coaches and speakers to use them as there seemed to be a dearth of reliable figures about business development for micro-businesses. I always said yes to those who wanted to use my figures, with the proviso that they had to mention my website as part of the credit. It's always been at the back of my mind to run the same survey again, to see if the results have changed since, as a measurable change in something over a number of years can also make a great news story.

New warning or advice

If you have expertise in something relevant to your audience, issuing some pertinent and timely advice or a warning can make a great story, especially if linked to a news hook. Think about headlines such as:

- With the Budget looming, local business expert warns that…
- Don't forget your pets on Bonfire Night says local pet shop
- 'Treat the ski slopes like the beach and don't forget your Factor 30', says top dermatologist

Exercise

What new warning or advice could you or your business offer?

Example

This last headline is genuine and one I developed when I had a private hospital well known for its dermatology department as a PR client. Dermatologists are in high demand from the media during the spring and summer to talk about how to look after your skin in the sun and on holiday, and then again in autumn to offer advice on how to look after your skin in cold weather.

I always struggled to get coverage for the dermatologists in the winter, however, and patient enquiries would drop. During a conversation a dermatologist happened to mention that he sees people every winter with moles and potential skin cancers on their foreheads. They're often keen skiers or ski instructors, because of the intense ultraviolet rays hitting the only part of their face or body that's not covered by protective clothing or goggles.

While it seems obvious advice, it was a message that wasn't being heard in the media, so we put a press release out with the headline above, offering new advice that was topical and relevant and definitely had human interest (we had a case study of a ski instructor who had been diagnosed with skin cancer the previous year by this dermatologist), so it was newsworthy. It got coverage in media outlets ranging from ski and extreme sport magazines and travel supplements to the health pages of *The Daily Telegraph* and a number of radio interviews, and drove an immediate spike in patient enquiries.

The even better news was that the following winter, a number of media outlets remembered this advice and came back and covered it again without us even lifting a finger.

New comment or opinion

This isn't dissimilar to offering warnings or advice as described above, but here you're looking to 'piggyback' on an existing story, offering a new opinion or comment that hopefully differs or stands out from the comments being offered by others.

To promote these types of stories you do need to keep a close eye on what is being covered in the media that is pertinent to your business and your audience. For example, is something being discussed in Parliament or by your local council? Has a celebrity said or done something you could comment on? Is there a new movie or game that is relevant to what you do?

Here are some examples of headlines you might look to emulate:

- 'No more red tape' says top business coach as Parliament debates new business regulations
- As council proposes new business centre, local business owner criticises 'lack of vision'
- As new *Star Wars* movie opens, safety expert calls for light-saber training classes for kids

Is it just me or is that last headline the story you'd read first?

If you want to comment on a story of the day, you need to move fast and get a press release out as early as possible. Journalists will be looking for expert commentators or new opinions for that day's news programmes and tomorrow's newspapers but, by lunchtime, they'll be pretty much sorted.

If you know of a story or news event that's coming up (the date of the Budget is known in advance, for instance) you can pre-prepare your comment, or even issue a comment release in advance, outlining what you'd like to see happen/announced, then put out another on the day reacting to what has been said. It's also worth approaching relevant journalists to ask if they're looking for expert input on forthcoming news events. For example, one friend who is a midwife and has written a book about birth, offers herself to media outlets in advance of royal births and often gets significant coverage.

The other great opportunity to offer comment or opinion is when your competitors have got a story running. Offer an alternative opinion, theory or option (rather than just saying 'they're terrible') and you're playing right into the media's desire for a bit of 'trouble'. Just be prepared for them to try to do the same to your stories.

Take a national story and make it local – or vice versa

If you're struggling to find a news story, look to the national news agenda for something relevant to your business and think about how you could make it relevant to your local media. A great way is to set yourself up as a local case study for what is happening nationally.

A press release along the lines of 'Local business among first to adopt new national guidelines' or 'National row affects local business' can get you local coverage while associating you as a national 'player'. It's also remarkable how quickly national media, desperate for a new human interest angle on a running story, will pick up on the local press coverage, so your national story made local might just make you national too.

Features

Once you've read the news stories at the front of a newspaper or magazine, you tend to come to the features. In broadcast media, features are the longer reports, discussions and even whole programmes away from the main news bulletins.

Features differ from news stories in a number of ways:

- They cover trends, background and details that don't fit in a news story.

- A feature will take a wider or deeper look at a topic, investigating it, considering different angles.

- They tend to be longer, more discursive and often reflect more of the personality (and opinion) of the journalist.

- Features are often more focused on human interest than on hard facts.

- Features don't have to be quite as timely or newsworthy as a news story. A feature could often have run last week or next month as they aren't necessarily as driven by topicality.

If you haven't got a news story to promote to the media, there may well be openings for you to take part in a feature instead. Do you or your business exemplify a current trend in society or in your industry? Are you part of 'the zeitgeist' or bucking the trends? Do you have some great case studies that aren't necessarily brand new but still have a good story to tell (and haven't been seen elsewhere already)?

Feature writers are often looking for interviewees, products to review, images to illustrate a feature, case studies, research and other resources. We'll discuss in the chapter about PR tools some of the ways you can get involved in features, especially using forward feature lists, and I'd encourage you to proactively seek out feature opportunities if you don't currently have anything new to talk about.

Pre-written features

Increasing numbers of local newspapers, trade publications and online outlets will now accept pre-written features for publication. This is largely a symptom of the dwindling number of journalists coupled with an increased demand for editorial content. It can be a great opportunity to get your message out there and especially position yourself as an expert in your topic.

Contact the publication you're targeting to ask if they will accept pre-written features and if so whether they have any guidelines on the topics they're interested in, the word count and their 'house style' of writing plus whether there is a deadline for submissions. Then stick to those guidelines, providing the feature they've requested at the length they've requested (within 20–30 words of their word count, not massively longer or shorter) by the date they've requested.

If you're suggesting features you think they might be interested in, ensure they offer real value for the reader and aren't just an advert for your business or product. Lots of media outlets like list features such as '10 top tips about X' or 'The five mistakes everyone makes about Y' so think about an eye-catching headline that offers an obvious incentive for the reader to read it.

You can even use the same pre-written feature in a number of different publications or outlets (especially online) but ensure you don't offer the same feature to competing or similar outlets, as they don't want their readers spotting the same feature elsewhere.

Exercise

What are your plans for generating PR coverage when you don't have anything newsworthy to talk about?

Ask 'So what?' before sending (or writing)
a press release. What media and you think
are news are probably two different things.

Rob Ashton
journalist

Getting your story out there – the press release

When you've identified a newsworthy story about your business that you want to promote to the media, you need a way of communicating that story to the journalists on your target media outlets. The best way to do that is by writing and distributing a press release.

You'll sometimes hear those in PR declare the death of the press release, saying that it's an outdated and an old-fashioned approach. I'm here to tell you that the press release is still very much alive and still the common currency of the PR world. If you ring, email or tweet a journalist to tell them about your story, nine times out of ten the first thing they'll ask is, 'Can you send me the press release?' Journalists often struggle to get out of the newsroom to attend events or press conferences and will usually ask to be sent the press release about what is being said or announced. Certainly in my role as a freelance journalist, I still receive the vast majority of story pitches and ideas in the form of press releases arriving in my email inbox.

A press release is simply a write-up of your story, written in a journalistic rather than a sales style. Its aim should be to communicate the main points of the story in a way that will make the journalist see the newsworthiness and relevance of your story to their publication and audience. It should give enough information for them to be able to write the story, but also make it clear what other elements are available from you to enhance the story, such as images, case studies, interviews and so on.

There are a few things that every press release needs:

The five W's: Who, What, Where, When and Why

Every time you write a press release you need to check that you have included all five W's, otherwise you have missed out a vital piece of information.

- Who: Who is this press release from? Which business has sent it out? Who is it about?

- What: What is this story about? What's happening? What is newsworthy about it? What makes it interesting, different, unusual?

- Where: Where is this story happening? Where, geographically, is this story relevant to?

- When: When is this event happening? When will this story be topical?

- Why: Why is this story important to the readers? Why will it make a difference to the lives of the readers? Why is this story happening now?

It's remarkable how often these basic pieces of information are missed out of a press release. Quite recently I received a press release about a launch event at a new gardening business. The writer managed to omit the name of the company, the venue of the event and the date. Did I go to the event or cover the story? No.

Exercise

What are the five W's of your story?

A headline

Your press release needs a clear, easy to understand headline that immediately hooks the readers in and makes it clear why this story is relevant to them.

Headline writing is a skill, but read the headlines in your target publication to get a feel for how they do it and try to match their 'house style'. For instance, if you're planning to pitch your story to a tabloid newspaper, you can use puns or humour in the way that they do, but if pitching to the *Financial Times*, you need your headline to have more gravitas and focus on business.

Think about how an advertising slogan is written – short, punchy, to the point. Some of the tricks of the advertising copywriter can be used such as alliteration, repetition and lists of three.

Let's say we're writing a press release about the launch of a new book about PR (which by the time you read this, I'll have done). Which of these headlines would entice you to want to know more?

- PR expert publishes new book about PR

- 'Can your business afford NOT to be doing public relations?' asks PR expert and author

- Get your name in the papers with PR top tips in brand new book out this week

I think the last of these is the strongest simply because it talks about the reader, not about the author, and tells them what they're going to get out of this story (and this book).

I quite often write a draft headline then come back and rewrite once I've written the press release, as often a form of words will suggest itself as I develop the copy of my release.

Exercise

Write a headline for your press release. Does it communicate quickly and clearly what the story is about, and will it make the journalist want to read more?

The most important information at the top

Most press releases never get read in full. They might get skimmed but in most cases the only part that will get read is the headline and possibly the first paragraph. This means that your first paragraph should aim to summarise the story, making it clear who and what it's about and why it's newsworthy and relevant. Even if the reader doesn't get beyond the first paragraph, they've picked up the main elements of the story.

So if I take the example I used above, my first paragraph might read:

> Businesses can now reach thousands of new customers via the media thanks to a new book, published this week, offering top tips on how to undertake PR from PR coach and journalist Steve Bustin. The book explains the processes businesses should undertake to raise their media profile and enable them to save thousands of pounds by doing their own PR rather than paying an agency to do it.

That captures all the necessary elements for a journalist on a business magazine, for instance, to know that this is relevant to their readers, is topical because it's out this week and how their readers will benefit from knowing about the book.

You should write the press release like a pyramid (Figure 1), with your headline being the summit of the pyramid, which you then broaden out to your first paragraph summary that includes all the most important information.

You then broaden that out again to the slightly less important information, and then again to go into background, history and other information that, if it doesn't get read, isn't essential to understanding the story.

Figure 1 How to structure the content in your press release

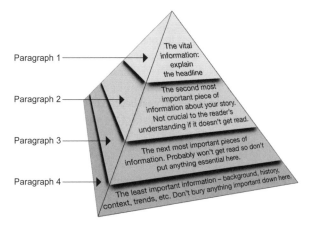

Paragraph 1 — The vital information: explain the headline

Paragraph 2 — The second most important piece of information about your story. Not crucial to the reader's understanding if it doesn't get read.

Paragraph 3 — The next most important pieces of information. Probably won't get read so don't put anything essential here.

Paragraph 4 — The least important information – background, history, context, trends, etc. Don't bury anything important down here.

Too often I see people turn this pyramid on its head and start their press release with something like, 'Our business was founded in 1974 and is based in Guildford and has 30 employees. We were founded by Mr Smith and…', and then the actual story (that this company is launching a really exciting new product that will make life better for millions of people) is buried down in about paragraph four. Guess what? Most journalists won't have bothered to read that far so will never have read the exciting news and as a result won't cover it.

> ### Exercise
>
> What information needs to be contained in the first paragraph? What can be 'relegated' to lower paragraphs?

Human interest

As discussed in a previous chapter, it's vital that you have some element of human interest in your story, to illustrate that whatever you're promoting will make a difference to the reader. Outline a case study or include a testimonial within your press release, ideally one that reflects the audience of the media outlet you're sending the release to.

Contacts

While your press release should contain all the pertinent information, a journalist may well want to know more, may want to ask questions or request an image or interview. You need to make that as easy as possible by including your contact details at the bottom of the release. Make sure you include an email address and a mobile number so that a journalist can contact you out of hours, as the media doesn't work 9–5.

Additional resources for journalists

Make it clear what else you're able to offer the journalist. This might include:

- Images. Attach a couple of images that illustrate the story but also outline what other images you have available.

Possibly include a link to a site where a range of high-quality images can be downloaded. Make sure your images are all high resolution (300dpi) and ideally professionally taken, not just a snap using a phone. Remember, this image may well become the defining image of your business so don't scrimp or waste the opportunity through lack of thought.

Good images to have available for the media include:

o Portrait shots of the main figures involved in the story, especially anyone quoted in the release. Aim for a background that gives these people context, not just a studio shot. Think about what they're wearing and the message that sends. Does the journalist really want yet another photo of yet another middle-aged man in a suit?

o If using a shot of a group of people, aim to make it more interesting than just a horizontal line of people. Something as simple as standing them up a staircase, or a shot taken looking down on them from above can make all the difference.

o A range of high-quality product shots if promoting a product, some 'cut out', i.e without any background.

o Screen shots need to be high resolution – a screen grab is not high enough quality for a print publication.

A really strong image can get a weaker story more coverage than a good story with a weak image. Be creative while remembering the context and message these images will send. I once got a client a third of a page of coverage in the *Financial Times* and the journalist admitted that it was the accompanying photo (taken in a mirrored lift with unusual reflections in the background and featured prominently) rather than the merit of the story that secured the coverage.

- Interviews with senior people and/or the main players in your story.

- Filming/recording opportunities. If you're pitching to TV, radio or a website, spell out what video or audio you have available to them or what filming/recording opportunities you can offer them. Broadcast journalists can only tell a story if there is something to look at or something to listen to. If you've got an opportunity for them to film something un-usual or visually interesting, let them know.

- Are you able to offer pre-filmed material, sometimes referred to as B-roll? Not all broadcasters will use it but if you've got broadcast quality, unedited video footage, you can make it available to broadcast media outlets.

- Additional case studies, especially if you have a range that fit different demographic audiences.

A few other pointers about how to make your press release stand out:

- Always write in the third person (they will..., they have an-nounced...), not in the first person (we are announcing..., we will be…).

- Write it as you'd like to see it appear in your target publica-tion, as if the journalist has written it, so giving *third-party* endorsement.

- Write it in the house style of the publication you're intending to send the release to. If you're writing for a magazine aimed at young women, it's going to have a very different tone to writing it for a trade publication. One style does not fit all. Read or listen to the media outlet to get a feel for the house style.

- Many press releases include a quote from a relevant spokesperson associated with the story, often the managing director or other senior figure. The quote is a useful way to add a more human note and possibly a slightly stronger sales message to the release. Many journalists dislike using these 'canned' quotes as the same quote can appear elsewhere, however. They would rather contact you to get their own quote from the person concerned.

- Avoid sales speak or anything that sounds or feels self-promotional. The journalist you want to write up this story is writing it to tell their audience about what's new, not to promote your business, so don't use any language that's too self-aggrandising.

- Avoid hyperbole and exaggeration. Is this product really 'groundbreaking'? Is it truly a UK first? Is it honestly the most exciting thing to emerge in this sector in years? Don't big yourself up too much but adopt the more measured, questioning tone of the journalist. If a journalist reads your release and it feels more like an advert than a news story, they'll hit the delete key very fast.

Working with a journalist: Alice Hart-Davis

Alice is a freelance journalist who writes about beauty and health for a range of national newspapers and magazines.

As a freelance journalist, I'm very open to stories from small businesses. In the beauty area there are an enormous number of tiny businesses starting up the whole time with very interesting, new ideas. They don't have the budget to advertise but these small players are important, so if something looks interesting, I'm happy to take a look at it.

As I'm a freelance, I'm independent. I don't work for magazines who only write about advertisers, so I can make a judgement about what I write about. Freelancers can be more approachable as they don't have to spend their time dealing with advertisers. I respond to most emails that come my way unless they're clearly a marketing gimmick, and if I say, 'I'll keep it on file', I really do, as it may not be right for me now but I keep everything as a searchable archive.

Drop me an email with a short, succinct introduction on why I should be interested in your product or service – sell it to me! I don't take stories from PRs any more seriously than direct from businesses.

Learn which journalists are interested in what things as every freelance journalist has their specialist area. Persistence really does pay, too. Always follow up as maybe the freelance journalist was busy when you first contacted them.

The anatomy of a press release

You will sometimes find press release templates offered for download online, where you literally fill in the blanks. I think using these is a mistake, as it encourages you to write a generic press release that won't stand out among the hundreds of press releases a journalist may receive every day.

While there are no absolute rules about how to format and write your press release, most follow a roughly similar format, which is worth working to, as this is how a journalist will expect to see the information laid out.

Layout for a typical press release

```
Media release

Today's date:

or

Diary date: (date of your story/event)


Headline

First paragraph. Sums up the entire story,
highlighting the most important information
that makes this story newsworthy.
```

Second paragraph. The next most important piece of information.

Third paragraph. The third most important piece of information.

Fourth paragraph. The least most important piece of information – background and so on.

Quote from someone important to the story, illuminating it and setting it in context.

Brief outline of case study/human interest element that illustrates the story.

Resource for the audience to find out more that you'd like the journalist to include – normally a web address. This is *not* where to put your personal contact details.

ENDS

[This tells the journalist that everything below this point is not for publication.]

Your contact details: email and phone number

List additional resources available to support this story such as images, filming opportunities and available interviewees

Notes for editors

[This is where you put deeper background – historical details, in-depth figures, full citations for any statistics or research you've quoted in the release, awards won in the past etc. This section is sometimes referred to as 'boilerplate' and rarely gets read. Anything of vital importance to the story should go further up the release.]

Now lets see how this would look in a sample press release, using the business development research story mentioned in the last chapter.

Sample press release

Media release

For immediate release: Thursday 24 February

Most successful business development tools for SMEs revealed: New research highlights referrals from clients as best strategy

New research by PR consultancy Vada Media (vadamedia.co.uk) published today has identified that the best business development approach for freelancers and micro-businesses offering professional or business services is to ask existing clients for referrals. 124 businesses took part in the study and these results offer a helping hand to freelancers and business owners unsure of where and how to invest time and money in the all-important quest for new business.

The key findings:

• 69% of the average freelancer's business is likely to come from recommendations and referrals made by existing clients and contacts.

• 94% of respondents cited recommendations from existing clients as the most important source of new work, with informal networking being mentioned by 88% of businesses.

• Websites were the third most important method for finding new clients, being mentioned by 82% of businesses surveyed.

• These were followed by professional bodies (47%), facilitated networking (groups such as BNI, 41%) and trade associations (35%).

• The more traditional 'cold' contact methods were far less popular, with email approaches being cited by only 31%, postal approaches by only 28% and telephone cold-calling by only 17% of businesses as an effective business development tool.

• Traditional advertising is successful for only 11%, with direct mail and online advertising each effective for only 6% of businesses.

The research was carried out by Vada Media, originally as part of an internal business planning exercise. The businesses that took part in the research represented the gamut of professional services including PR, fundraising, advertising, photography, copywriting, event management, web development, accountancy and marketing. 47% of those surveyed were sole traders, 18% were individuals registered as a limited company and 35% were limited companies with more than one employee.

Steve Bustin, Managing Director of Vada Media said the results held useful pointers for other businesses offering professional services:

This research was designed as part of an internal business development exercise, but as the results were collated it became obvious that the findings would be of use to many other businesses. The results prove that the best way to find those all-important new clients is to canvass current clients for referrals plus invest time in informal and formal networking. So don't be shy, ask your clients about who they might be able to refer you to.

CASE STUDY

David Stephens is a freelance designer based in Brighton who took part in the survey. He says that proactively asking existing clients for referrals has revolutionised his business:

I've gone to plenty of networking events and while I've made some useful contacts it's very much a slow burn in terms of generating leads as it's about developing relationships. A business coach suggested to me that I should start asking existing clients for referrals and it's been a revelation. My clients (who are, thankfully, all very happy with my work) actually seem quite pleased to be asked and have either made personal introductions to people they know or have said that now they know I'm looking for clients, will bear me in mind if they hear of anyone looking for a designer. Interestingly, a couple of clients said they hadn't bothered referring potential work as they'd assumed I was fully booked. Needless to say, it's something I'll continue to do from time to time.

ENDS

For more information about Vada Media, the business development research or interviews with Steve Bustin, call 020 7183 1096 (diverts to mobile out of hours) or email steve@vadamedia.co.uk.

Notes for editors

• PR consultancy Vada Media was founded in 2002 and represents clients in sectors including health care, aesthetics, business services and the arts.

• The raw data from the research is available in spreadsheet form for those requiring more detail.

Who should you send your press release to?

Once you've written your press release, you need to think carefully about which journalists you're going to send it to.

Identifying your target audience

Before you even do that, however, think about who you would like to read about your business in a paper or magazine. What type of customer would you like to hear about your story on their favourite radio station or on their 'must read' blog?

If you don't already have one, build up a profile of your perfect customer or client.

If they are individuals think about:

- Where do they live? Is their location important to your business?
- What age and gender are they?
- What sort of job do they do? Is that important?
- What are their interests and hobbies?
- What media do they consume? What do they read, click on, watch and listen to?

If your customer is another business, think about:

- What type(s) of business do I want to reach?
- What size of business?
- What sector?
- Where are they based? Is their location important?
- Who within that business do I need to reach? A specific role or department?
- What media might someone in that role consume as part of their professional lives?
- What media might that person also consume in their personal life?

You might need to build more than one profile for more than one type of customer, which in turn may need more than one press release to go to more than one sector of the media. As I said earlier, one size doesn't fit all.

Exercise

Build a profile of your ideal customer(s), whether they are consumers or businesses and business people.

Once you've developed your customer profile, you can start to think in more depth about the media that person might consume. Occasionally you might need to make a generalisation (for example, if you want to reach 'white van man' then you might need to make an assumption that they're more likely to read a tabloid newspaper than a broadsheet).

How might you find out what media your ideal customers consume? The best way is often simply to ask. Ask existing customers who fit a similar profile what they read, watch or listen to. It can be a great question to ask at the beginning or end of a meeting or customer interaction, or add a survey question to an email. If you're going to a meeting with a business client, look at which trade magazines and newspapers are on the coffee table in reception. If this client reads those publications, it's highly likely that similar companies that you want to reach do so, too.

Try searching online for media that fits your target audience such as 'news websites for accountants', 'gardening magazines' or 'radio programmes about the arts'. If you're targeting consumers, go into a large newsagent and browse through the myriad titles to find the ones that serve your audience.

Start to build up a list of the newspapers, magazines, trade press, websites, radio and TV programmes your target customer is likely to be consuming on a regular basis. If you want to get yourself and your business in front of these people, this is now your target media list.

Exercise

Draw up a target media list based on the media outlets your ideal customers will be consuming. Include at least one newspaper, one magazine, one radio programme/station, one TV programme and one website.

Which journalist should you send your release to?

Once you know which media outlet you're going to target, you need to think about which journalist on that outlet you're going to contact.

Your first step is to do some research. Pick up the publication or visit its website and start reading it. Which journalists are writing about stories or businesses similar to your own? Do certain journalists have certain roles or specialisms? If the journalist's contact details aren't listed in the publication, they almost certainly will be on the associated website (search for the 'contact us' page).

If you can't find the email address for a particular journalist, you can normally work out what it will be by looking at any other published email addresses and copying the same format such as firstname.surname@ or initial.surname@. For example, *The Guardian* outlines the correct email format and gives email addresses for many of the departments you may want to contact on their website at theguardian.com/help/contact-us

There's also a very useful, free website, media.info, which lists most of the mainstream media outlets in the UK (newspapers, magazines, radio, TV and their online versions) and includes many of the journalists and their specialisms plus their email addresses, phone numbers and the like. If you're really serious about PR there are also a number of subscription services that update their contacts database regularly and allow you to run full searches and build extensive media contact lists. Search CisionPoint or Gorkana for details.

Try to find as specific an email address as possible, ideally for an individual journalist, as generic emails such as news@ or editorial@ are inundated with press releases, so it's much harder to make your news story stand out. While an individual journalist is still likely to receive hundreds of releases, they'll be much more tuned in to the stories likely to be relevant to them.

Even relatively small media outlets are likely to have a number of journalists, all with their own specialism. For example, the website for my local paper lists the following:

- Editor
- Website editor
- Two assistant new editors

- Head of content
- Chief reporter
- Two senior reporters
- Health reporter
- Business reporter
- Crime reporter
- Local government reporter
- Three reporters
- Sports desk
- Picture desk
- The guide (events listings)

So who do I send my release to? It depends on my story. If it's a business story, clearly the business reporter is the right person. How about if I run a health-related business? I could also send it to the health reporter. If I've got a great image I'll send it to the picture desk, but if it's a more general story I'll send it to the assistant news editors or a senior reporter.

Should I always pitch to the most senior journalist?

It might be tempting to think that the best journalist to contact is the one right at the top, the editor. I think that's a mistake as the editor overseas the entire publication or broadcast outlet. They consider the overall shape of each edition and rarely actually write stories except on the smallest publications. They're highly unlikely to have the time to read your press release or speak to you on the phone.

If you can't find a journalist with the right specialism, or you're just not sure who to contact, I'll often call a publication and ask to speak to the editorial assistant. This is normally the most junior person in the newsroom or office, and while this certainly doesn't mean they are the least busy, they are often easiest to reach and most willing to give you some time on the phone. They'll also often be able to suggest the best person on the team to contact and sometimes even make an introduction to that person for you.

What about freelance journalists?

Not every journalist whose work appears in a particular media outlet will actually work there. More and more journalists now work freelance and usually get paid per story they write.

There can be some major advantages to pitching your story to a freelance journalist. First, that journalist may well write for a number of publications and a canny freelance may be able to write different versions of your story for different outlets, so (a) they earn more money and (b) you get more coverage. Secondly, freelancers may be able to help you to hone your story to make it more newsworthy, as this helps them pitch it to the editors who commission them. Finally, freelancers can be much longer-term contacts as, unlike staff journalists, they don't tend to get promoted or move to another publication and disappear off your radar.

Try searching online (especially on LinkedIn or Twitter) for 'business freelance journalists' or any other specialism and you'll find lists of suitable journalists. Take the time to get to know what they write about and who they write for, to make sure your story is likely to be right for them.

How do you 'pitch' to journalists?

I've already used the term 'pitch' several times so we should explore what that means.

Pitching to a journalist simply means alerting them to your story in some way. There are a number of ways you can do it.

Email

- Always copy and paste the text of your press release into the body of the email. Don't send it as an attachment as most journalists won't open it, either for reasons of time or because they don't want to risk opening something that might contain a virus.

- Make sure your headline is also the email subject line so even without opening it the journalist can see that this is relevant to them and their publication. I regularly receive a press release from one of the major seed and plant mail order companies that simply says 'Press release' in the subject line then has no text in the email, just an attached Word document. I have no idea what it's about and have never opened the attachments so I've never covered their stories.

- Send the press release to one journalist, not to a long BCC list (or even worse, a CC list). If a journalist can see or suspects that the same story has gone to all their colleagues or competitors, they're far less likely to cover it. They want something unique to them, not the same old stuff that everyone else has got.

- You don't need to open your email with 'Dear Steve, I hope you are well and had a lovely weekend' – unless you actually know the journalist personally. Get straight to the point.

Phone

- If you're a confident cold-caller, by all means hit the phone and ring all your target journalists. Expect a lot of voicemails and gatekeepers, but if done with the confidence that you've got a great story that this journalist is going to be happy to be alerted to, it can be a very effective strategy.

- Similarly to email, don't waste time on platitudes. As soon as you've introduced yourself, ask if now is a good time to talk. If a journalist is on deadline they'll appreciate you showing consideration, but ask when would be a good time to call back. If they're OK to talk, pitch your story briefly and concisely, playing up the newsworthy elements.

- If this is the first (or only) journalist you have pitched to, say so, as if you're willing to give it to that outlet as an exclusive (that is, you don't mention it to anyone else) then they may be more likely to cover it, as every journalist loves to have something their competitors don't.

- Be prepared for the journalist you call to simply ask you to email them the press release. Yes, this is partly a tactic to get you off the phone, but it gives you a chance to double-check you have the correct email address for them and also means that when it hits their inbox, the subject line is familiar and they're more likely to open it.

Should you email and phone?

This is one of the most disputed topics among journalists and public relations practitioners. Should you call a journalist after you've sent them the press release by email, to check whether they've seen it?

Most journalists will say you shouldn't, as if they want to cover the story they'll contact you, and you're just wasting their time because they do at least glance at every press release that comes into their inbox.

Most people who've done some PR will tell you, however, that remarkably often a journalist you've rung to chase will say, 'No, I've not seen that, can you send it again?' Now they're primed to receive it and the occasions that that has led to getting coverage make it worth the risk of annoying them with that call.

Personally, I think you should only call the top three or four journalists on your key target list, but always have something additional to offer them – some extra images, case studies or interviews, so there is some benefit to them in taking your call.

Social media

Journalists *love* social media. They're all over most platforms, especially Twitter, as it's a great place to find stories, interviewees, experts and the like.

Find and follow your key journalists on Twitter. You'll soon get to know more about them, what they write about and the sorts of stories they're looking for. They may well use Twitter to ask for stories or to request specific information or resources.

Try to engage with these journalists and build a relationship with them. Retweet them. Reply to them. Offer help, even if it doesn't result in coverage. Make yourself visible and useful to them and they may well follow you back.

By all means pitch to them on social media, too. I know some journalists who will only accept pitches via Twitter, so could you sum up your story in 140 characters? When undertaking PR I will often tweet a journalist to ask if they'd be interested in a certain type of story. If they say they are, I'll ask for the best email address and then they're primed to receive my story in their inbox. As a journalist I like it when people contact me on Twitter or LinkedIn to sound me out about a story as it means I can educate them on what types of stories work for me (and keep my email inbox that bit clearer).

Other ways to pitch

Once upon a time, PR was all about the fax machine. I remember the fax machine in the corner of the BBC radio newsroom that used to spew out press releases constantly, into a large metal bin immediately underneath it. No one ever read them because they weren't addressed to anyone.

If you've got a product that you'd like to get in front of a journalist, send it by post or even deliver it by hand. Any journalist who writes about products, such as tech, fashion or beauty, will receive a bulging mailbag every day.

Try pitching in person, too. If you're at a conference or trade show, track down the journalists who are attending. Trade magazines will often have a stand, or go and find the press office. Meeting someone face to face makes it much more likely they'll remember you next time you email them a story idea.

Timing your pitches

There are a few questions I'm always asked about pitching a story or sending a press release.

- Is there a good time to pitch?

  This is a tricky one as every journalist will be working to different deadlines (especially as news is a 24/7 business), but try to avoid pitching to them when they are close to deadline as they are only focused on the stories already in front of them. If you're not sure if they're on deadline – ask. For daily newspapers or broadcasters, I'd suggest pitching mid-morning, when they'll have had their editorial meetings but aren't too close to their late afternoon deadline.

Make sure you pitch in plenty of time for a certain edition or issue. For example, most weekly local newspapers come out on a Friday morning, so don't pitch it on Thursday afternoon, as you'll have missed the deadline. Monthly publications can have a lead time of two or even three months so prepare early. Broadcasters have more 'rolling' deadlines but if you're pitching to a live programme, don't pitch immediately before they go on air or while they're broadcasting.

- How often should you pitch?

Don't become part of the wallpaper. For several years when I was writing weekly news stories for *The Pink Paper*, I would receive a press release every single week from a well-known HIV charity, normally with a really weak story. This felt like pestering for coverage and in the end I redirected their mails into my spam folder. I might have missed the occasional good story but it got them off my back.

For most businesses I suggest having one story a quarter to put out as a press release. That's regular enough to keep you on a journalist's radar but not often enough for you to become repetitive. Obviously if a time-critical story suddenly presents itself you should put it out, but aim for a few great stories rather than regular weaker stories. A journalist can't keep covering the same businesses, so don't risk them covering a weaker story in one edition (perhaps in a quiet news week) then feeling unable to cover a much better story soon after, for fear of looking repetitive.

- Can I use a web service or newswire to send my press release?

This is the lazy, scattergun approach to sending a press release. I've yet to meet a journalist who has to go searching on these websites for stories as they're inundated with press releases every day. Save your money, do your homework and target your key journalists yourself.

- Can I insist on copy approval before publication?

In a word, no. If you've bought an advertorial then you'll get copy approval, but otherwise once you've sent your release, you don't have control over how your story is written up. Occasionally a journalist might ask you to check what they've written for accuracy, especially if it's a very specialist or technical topic, but you don't control what the journalist has written so please don't ask to see or approve it before it's published.

- Should I invite the journalists to a press conference or event as part of my pitch?

Most media outlets work on very small teams and journalists often struggle to attend events, unless it's being held by a big brand and well-known name. If you're holding an event anyway, by all means invite your key journalists, but don't organise a press event and expect journalists to want to come to hear about your story in return for a free glass of wine. Likewise leave the PR stunts to the big brands and agencies that have money to burn, unless you're confident you can create a great picture or filming opportunity on very little budget.

- Should I pitch to bloggers?

If they write about your type of story or business and their blog is read by your target audience, yes, pitch to them in exactly the same way you would a journalist on a more traditional media outlet.

Working with a journalist: Peter Lindsay

Peter is the business reporter on the Brighton *The Argus.*

I'm always on the lookout for good business stories but it has to be a news story rather than just a puff for the company. I'm not going to take your press release seriously if it basically says, 'We are a wonderful company.'

I'm interested in stories about a business or about the business community. It needs to have a news angle, something that interests people. It's got to be something with a bit of wow, a bit different. We get huge numbers of emails so your press release has got to be something that makes us stop and think, 'That's of note, that's something the public will be interested in.'

Look at any local newspaper and you'll notice that most of the stories are photo led, so if you have a good, powerful image, that's going to make a huge difference immediately. No story ever appears on our website without a photograph.

Geography is important. Being in Brighton we wouldn't cover a company in Portsmouth, for example, as it's out of our patch. We delete press releases from all over the country, as we're only interested in Sussex with a focus on Brighton and Hove.

A local paper is read by consumers so we're interested in people stories. People like to read positive stories such as new jobs being created. People think we only report bad news but that's not the case. Job gains are as interesting as job losses, because both affect people.

Send your story in by email with a good image, not too many words and make sure you have an eye-catching headline, so it makes a good first impression and really stands out.

Working with a journalist: Guy Clapperton

Guy Clapperton is the editor of *Intelligent Sourcing* magazine, formerly *Professional Outsourcing* magazine

Our magazine is really focused on big name companies but our online news feed will cover smaller businesses, although they need something good to say.

A good story from a small business would be about someone or something that is disrupting the market we serve and could really make a difference to our readership in their daily lives and work. I'm not interested in 'X wins big new contract' but if this new contract is indicative of a big change or something wider going on in the industry, I'm interested.

I'm really interested in changes in trends – is something on the way in or way out? What are the business implications? Don't tell me about how the industry is now but what is going to change the industry in six months or two years so my readers can prepare for that change.

A trade or industry specialist magazine aims to be an independent voice and source of what's going on, without any vested interests. We tell you what people are actually saying, so case studies and spokespeople are always welcome, although spokespeople must be experts with current industry experience.

> *I do read press releases as they're indispensable for our daily news feed but I'm aware that everyone will have the same story. I tend to prefer emails but if someone wants to approach me via LinkedIn or Facebook, that's fine too.*

Routinely look at whatever your business is doing to identify what is happening that's new, different and/or exciting. If it is something which has impact on your local community, your business community, your region, your country or the world then it is worth telling the appropriate media outlet.

Michael Dodd
journalist

Getting coverage – know what people are saying about you

Sending your first press release out is an exciting moment, as suddenly you're putting a story about some aspect of your business into the big wide world.

Hitting 'send' on your email can be a slightly deflating experience, however, as you won't necessarily get any immediate response, particularly if your release was for a diary date some time in advance. A journalist won't necessarily let you know if they're covering your story either, especially if your press release was so well written and had such great quotes and photos that they don't need anything else from you in order to cover the story. Take that as a compliment. There have even been occasions when a time-stretched journalist has copied and pasted my press release straight into their publication, which I take to be an even bigger compliment (although I suspect it had a lot to do with them not having time to rewrite it).

As soon as you've sent out your press release, make sure you have the mechanisms in place to catch any mentions of you or your story. Here are a few to use:

- Google Alerts (google.co.uk/alerts) is a free service run by Google that will email you every time a word or term you want to keep an eye on is picked up by Google's search bots. You can set up as many as you like, so you can have them searching on your name or that of your spokesperson, your business name, a product name or even a competitor's name. I have one set up on my name, my business name and the title of my previous book. One caveat, though. Google Alerts is far less rigorous than it used to be and seems to miss a lot of mentions of keywords. It was rumoured that it might become a pay service but there's no sign of that happening (fortunately), or of its efficacy being improved (unfortunately).

- Mention (mention.com) seems to be much better at picking up… mentions. It works in a similar way to Google Alerts although on their free plan you're only allowed to set up one alert that will pick up a maximum of 100 mentions of that search term a month. Their paid plans offer a lot more flexibility and analytics. If nothing else, set up your one free alert on your business name as their hit rate for spotting mentions seems to be much better than Google Alerts.

- Talkwalker Alerts (talkwalker.com/en/alerts) seems to be the best of both worlds, offering good results and as many free alerts as you want. I have all three of these services running as occasionally one will pick up something the others have missed.

- Track social media. There are numerous tools that will track, measure and analyse your social media pages and profiles for you but, if nothing else, make sure you run regular searches for your keywords and phrases, especially when you've just put out a press release. Someone may post about your story without tagging you in the post so you won't necessarily get a notification.

- Buy the publication, listen to the programme, search the website and generally keep an eye out for any coverage. This might sound obvious but it always amazes me how many businesses undertaking PR don't actually buy or subscribe to (let alone read) the publications they're targeting. Clearly you can't read every newspaper or magazine but make sure you're actively monitoring your five top target media outlets.

- Use a clippings or media monitoring service. There are a number of media monitoring services around who really do read pretty much every publication (well, they've got robots that scan most of them but some are still searched by real people) and they'll email you even the smallest mention of you or your story based on keywords. Most are subscription services and can be pricey, especially if they charge per clipping. Check out Gorkana or Meltwater if you think it might be useful to you, but I particularly like Coverage Book (coveragebook.com), which creates clippings books from weblinks, complete with measurement metrics.

One caveat – if you're going to start collecting and especially reproducing clippings (such as on your website), you may need a licence from the Newspaper Licensing Authority (nlamediaaccess.com) and/or The Copyright Licensing Agency (cla.co.uk) for magazines. Check their websites for details of what they cover and whether you need a licence.

Send out a clear, succinct press release outlining USP and make sure spelling and grammar is correct if you want to be taken seriously. No frills or fancy stuff necessary – just the relevant facts with website and contact details that include a direct phone number, not just an email.

Pattie Barron
journalist

Tools for building your PR campaign

There are a wide range of tools available to help you build your campaign. Some require a certain level of investment, but for those listed below I consider the cost to be absolutely worth it. I should point out that I'm not on commission with any of the companies who make or run any of the tools I'm about to suggest; I just think they're useful to anyone planning and running a PR campaign.

Most of these tools mean that you know what journalists and media outlets are looking for in advance, putting you ahead of most other businesses with whom you might be competing for column inches or air time.

The free tool: #JournoRequest

This is a hashtag used by journalists looking for information and input for features and news stories. It's predominantly used on Twitter although it does also get used on Facebook and Instagram.

Search on Twitter for #journorequest and you'll find a long and fairly fast moving stream of requests. These can be from any media outlet on pretty much any topic, so it can be worth adding a suitable keyword (such as 'business') to your search to narrow it down a little. Just a glance at the stream as I write reveals requests from journalists in the last hour for a menswear expert, someone to comment about account-based marketing in the B2B space, a woman who is badly affected by air pollution and a national newspaper looking for a social media expert to comment on using social media to boost sales in the run-up to Christmas, among about a dozen other requests. Could any of those have been applicable to you or your business?

It would be virtually impossible to read and evaluate every request that comes through but it's well worth dipping in regularly to keep an eye out for suitable requests. It's also a great way to find journalists who write about topics that are pertinent to your business, who you can follow and engage with. Even if a certain request isn't right for you, if you can help that journalist by suggesting someone else they should talk to, it's going to start a very positive conversation between you and them.

Case study: #JouroRequest

David Vallance runs Glasgow-based digital agency Digital Impact and gets media coverage by tracking the JournoRequest hashtag.

We've found the online journalist requests to be a good way to get placements in really good quality publications such as The Daily Telegraph *and* The Guardian *but also on blogs and websites such as* B2B Marketing *magazine and Virgin's entrepreneur site.*

We cast the net pretty wide looking for opportunities that demonstrate our skills, so we look for enquiries about digital expertise, cybersecurity and anything in our remit that shows off what makes our company unique and special. We also contribute to business stories about business culture, recruitment, training etc.

We don't watch the hashtag for particular outlets but the volume of requests is low enough for us to consider everything. We're seeing both brand recognition and great SEO results as a result of the coverage we get, with people telling us they saw us in the papers. Getting content in publications is now very much part of our regular marketing activity and using the JournoRequest hashtag sits alongside more traditional PR, putting out press releases when we've got a good story.

The time and effort you need to put in is so miniscule it would be criminal not to be doing it!

Response Source

If there is one tool worth paying for to boost your PR campaign it's this one, especially if you're keen to get into national media.

Response Source (responsesource.com) is a subscription service that allows you to receive requests from journalists on a huge range of topics. Unlike #journorequest, however, these requests are properly streamed and filtered. You subscribe to topic 'categories' so you will only receive requests that are pertinent to that particular sector. The quality of requests tends to be much higher than on the hashtag, too.

There are currently 25 categories, from Business & Finance and Construction & Property to Retail & Fashion, Home & Garden and Women's Interest & Beauty. The categories are priced according to how busy they are, from around £400 per year for Farming & Animals to nearer £900 for Consumer Technology (obviously these prices can change). That might seem like a major investment for a small business, but if it secures you just one piece of good coverage during that year, it can pay for itself very quickly; and compare it to the cost of buying an advert.

Requests from journalists can be for anything: interviewees, expert guests, case studies, products to review; images; competition prizes; locations for photo shoots; background briefings; or even just story ideas. It's widely used by national newspapers, freelance journalists, consumer magazines, trade press, TV and radio journalists and producers and increasing numbers of bloggers. Even if an enquiry isn't relevant to your business, you'll soon start to get a feel for who is writing about what topic.

I've seen small businesses gain coverage in everything from the *Financial Times* to ITV's *This Morning* thanks to a Response Source enquiry. They offer a week's free trial and their team are very good at helping you pick the right categories for your business sector or the keywords you're interested in. One word of warning: the busier categories (such as the Women's Interest & Beauty) can be *very* busy. When I was running my PR business and was a subscriber to two or three categories, I could receive 40 or more requests a day, which can seem slightly overwhelming. The quieter (and cheaper) categories may only generate half a dozen enquiries a week but they'll be very focused.

I'm not on their payroll (honest) but if you're serious about doing PR for your business, I think this is a must have.

Case study: Response Source

Jennifer Earle runs Chocolate Ecstasy Tours who provide guided walking tours of London's chocolate shops (chocolateecstasytours.com). She started using Response Source in 2013, subscribing to the Food & Drink category.

I receive about 50 journalist enquiries a week via Response Source. They're not all relevant to me and it can be challenging to even read them all let alone reply to those that are relevant, so occasionally I miss opportunities if I'm out on tours, due to the journalists having short deadlines.

Those enquiries are responsible for almost all our PR coverage in the last few years. I replied to an enquiry from Good Housekeeping *who were looking for a case study of a woman who had 'felt the fear and done it anyway' and when the coverage appeared my sales were more than double the same month the year before.*

I've also appeared in Woman *and* Prima *magazines in features about women in business and the coverage led to my best sales months that year.*

I never cut and paste my response to a journalist enquiry, even if it would save me time. I tend to look at the magazine or website to make sure I'm making it as relevant as possible and look up the journalist to see what I can find out about them. I write one or two short paragraphs, give them a link to my high-res images and offer to send them a press release. I'll also invite them to come on a tour although they often don't have time to come.

HARO: Help A Reporter Out

HARO (helpareporter.com) is very similar to Response Source but has a much more international reach. They send out enquiries in batches three times a day. They do have some UK enquiries, but not nearly as many as Response Source. If you were looking to reach international media, though, it could be worth investigating.

AskCharity

AskCharity (charitycomms.org.uk/askcharity) works in the same way as Response Source and HARO but is aimed at charities, campaigning groups and social enterprises.

Forward feature lists

Wouldn't it be lovely if publications told you in advance what they're going to write about? Some publications do, by issuing forward feature lists, sometimes referred to as editorial diaries or advanced feature lists.

It tends to be trade and specialist magazines that issue forward feature lists, rather than consumer titles, but if you're looking to gain coverage in B2B titles, they are well worth investigating. As we discussed in an earlier chapter, getting coverage in a feature is a great way to keep your profile high when you don't have a news story to talk about.

Magazines issue these diaries primarily because they want to let advertisers know what they're going to be covering over the next 12 months, in the hope those advertisers will want to buy ads alongside relevant editorial. They are incredibly useful PR tools, however.

You'll find them on the publication's website. Google 'forward feature lists' and the year you're interested in, and you'll find dozens come up. It's often included in the 'Advertise with us' section, sometimes described as the 'media pack'. Most publications issue their list for next year in about October or November of the current year, although some are now starting to publish rolling 12-month feature lists.

Most forward feature lists will outline the topics that every issue in a year is going to cover, although it's normally just a brief description. Here are some real examples.

From a November issue of a travel industry magazine:

- Latin America
- All-inclusive Holidays

- Globes Voting Supplement
- River Cruise Supplement

From the September issues (across four weeks) of a magazine aimed at grocery trade and shop owners:

- Focus On: Hot Beverages
- Focus On: Sauces & Condiments
- Special: 150 UK Supplier Rankings
- Guide to: Snacking
- Focus On: Spirits
- Special: Independent View
- Special: The Dairymen Supplement
- Focus On: Sports Nutrition & Energy
- Special: The Green Issue
- Guide to: Franchise & Fascia

From the February issues (across four weeks) of a magazine aimed at the property sector:

- 5 February:
  - London Supplement
  - West Midlands
- 12 February:
  - Occupiers
  - Surrey & Sussex
- 19 February:
  - Sheds supplement
  - Kent
  - Property salary survey

- 26 February:
    - Retail, Leisure & Hotels Supplement
    - Bristol and the South West

If your business supplies sheds, or fits out garden offices, or supplies domestic security equipment, knowing that a magazine read by your trade customers is running a supplement all about sheds in mid-February is incredibly useful intelligence. It would be a great place for your business to be covered as it's going to be read by those interested in supplying or fitting out sheds.

Acting on this intelligence requires a slightly different approach to sending out a news story, however. Features are planned on a longer-term basis and the deadlines are much earlier. For example, the deadline for the feature to be finished is often three to four weeks before publication for a weekly magazine. The journalist writing that feature, whether in-house or freelance, will be starting their planning several weeks before that, looking out for products, experts and opinions to feature.

If you want to be in the 19 February sheds supplement, say, you need to be getting on the journalist's radar in early January or even mid-December. For monthly magazines you probably need to start two to three months before publication, bearing in mind that the November issue will often appear in mid October.

Your approach should initially be to the features editor and their contact details are often listed on the forward feature list. Don't pitch straight to them, though, as it's unlikely to be them writing the feature. Ask them who *is* writing the feature and if there's any guidance on what they're going to be covering. The features editor may well give you the email address for the journalist concerned.

Email the writer of the feature with a short, focused email on who you are, what your business does and what you can offer. Do you, for instance, have some great case studies showing why metal sheds are better than wooden ones? Do you have some great images of sheds *in situ* or perhaps a video of a shed being erected, if you're pitching to an online publication? Basically, make yourself useful to the journalist without giving them the hard sell. They may well be very grateful that you've just made their life a lot easier and given them access to materials they were otherwise going to have to search for.

A few hours spent searching for relevant features that you could contribute to can be a great way to start building a pipeline of coverage.

Expert Sources

Expertise is in demand by the media. Journalists are always looking for new voices to bring their reports to life, either explaining something complex in easy to understand terms or offering an opinion on the topic at hand.

Promoting yourself as a media expert, a potential interviewee or guest is another great tool in your PR arsenal. Journalists will often go back to the same people time and time again, partly because they are (hopefully) good interviewees but also because they're easy to get hold of and happy to help.

If you'd like journalists to call you rather than your competitor when they need an expert to interview, you need to put yourself out there. Make sure your website and social media profiles say that you are available for interview and link to any coverage that proves your expertise or shows you in action.

There's also an excellent directory of media experts. Expert Sources (expertsources.co.uk) allows journalists to search by keyword for experts on all sorts of topics, from academics to those representing charities to business owners with expertise in a particular sector or industry.

You set up a profile on the site (from around £120 per year) listing your areas of expertise and the topics you're available to speak on. You can add keywords at any time so if a story comes on to the news agenda that you feel you can comment on, you can add all the relevant keywords immediately.

I know people who've picked up regular media 'gigs', and even paid appearances, as a result of having a profile on the site.

Media interview training

If you are serious about raising your profile in the media, especially if you're promoting yourself as a media expert, get yourself some media training. Even if you're just putting out press releases, it's worth getting yourself trained up in the skills necessary to give great interviews.

Whether you're talking to your local paper or Radio 4's *Today* programme, interviews can be tricky, and not knowing how to communicate your key messages effectively can leave you open to going completely 'off message' and potentially doing more harm than good. Not all journalists are going to 'do a Paxman' and try to trip you up, but they are there to ask the questions they think their readers or listeners would ask, even if those aren't the questions you want to be asked.

Top tips for media interviews

If you're asked to undertake a media interview, a few things to consider beforehand:

- What role am I playing in this interview? Am I talking about my own story, commenting on someone else's story (expressing an opinion) or am I there to explain something I am an expert in to a 'layman' audience?

- What's the key message I want to get across in this interview? If the audience remember one thing of what I say, what do I want it to be?

- What sort of language is appropriate for this media outlet? How simple do I need to keep it?

- What sort of questions is the journalist likely to ask me? Write down 5 likely questions and try answering them.

- What's the worst question they could ask me? How could I answer it?

- Don't learn answers so you can parrot them. An interview (especially for broadcast media) is a conversation between you and the journalist, so just chat to the person asking the questions.

- Who could run a mock interview with me? Ask a colleague or a friend to play the role of a journalist and ask you your likely questions.

- Do I need media training before I go in front of a microphone or camera, to minimise the risk of saying something I shouldn't?

See the Reading list (page 95) at the end of this book for some good guides to giving effective media interviews.

There are plenty of media trainers around (including me!). Search online for a trainer who is also a current or former journalist. They will help you to develop the messages you want to get across and put you through your paces with mock interviews in a range of different styles. Seeing yourself on camera being put under pressure by an interviewer isn't always comfortable but it's great practice for the real thing.

It amazes me how often a business owner will put themselves forward for an interview and believe that they can 'busk it', saying that they don't need any training for something that could be seen by millions of people. Just search for 'interviewee fail' on YouTube to see quite how badly that can go.

Exercise

Which tools are you going to use in your PR campaign? Who's going to manage them?

Have a plan – build a PR strategy

It's very easy to start your PR activity full of enthusiasm and good intentions but for it to drop down your to-do list very fast, especially if you've had a couple of false starts. This is why you need to embed PR into your marketing and business development planning.

If you've been making notes and trying the exercises as you've worked through this book, you already have the start of a PR strategy document, but if you'd like a basic PR strategy template, you can download it from bit.ly/PRStrategyTemplate

The template is formatted as a series of questions to answer but here's what your strategy should have in it.

An analysis of your current and recent PR

- What PR activity have you undertaken?
- What worked well?
- What didn't work – and why?
- What are your competitors doing in terms of PR?
- Is there anything you can learn from their activities?

An analysis of your public perception and reputation

- What do your key audiences currently know or understand about your business?
- Is it accurate?
- Is it positive or negative?
- What do you need to change?

What do you want PR to achieve for your business?

- Measurable objective 1:
- Measurable objective 2:
- Measurable objective 3:

Who are your target audiences?

- B2B or business-to-consumer (B2C)?
- Profile of target audience 1:
- Profile of target audience 2:
- Profile of target audience 3:

For each target audience, define your key media targets:

- National newspapers:
- Local/regional newspapers:
- Consumer magazines:
- Trade/professional magazines:
- Online outlets:
- Broadcast outlets:

Who is the key journalist you want to reach at each of those media outlets?

- National newspapers:
- Local/regional newspapers:
- Consumer magazines:
- Trade/professional magazines:
- Online outlets:
- Broadcast outlets:

What are the news stories you can offer to these key media targets and when?

- Story 1:
  - Target date for coverage:
  - When does it need to be released?
- Story 2:
  - Target date for coverage:
  - When does it need to be released?
- Story 3:
  - Target date for coverage:
  - When does it need to be released?

What other resources do you have to support each story?

- Images:
- Video:
- Case studies:
- Filming opportunities:

- Interviewees:
- Other:

What other tools are you going to use to further your PR campaign?

- Tool 1:
- Tool 2:
- Tool 3:

How often are you going to evaluate the success of your PR campaign and adjust your tactics and schedule as needed?

- Monthly:
- Quarterly:
- Annually:
- Other:

What constitutes success for this campaign?

- Have you met your measurable objectives outlined earlier in your plan?
- Did you have other goals or outcomes in mind and, if so, have you met them?
- What results would you be pleased with?

Timeline

A timeline is an important part of planning and carrying out your PR campaign, especially as different types of media outlet have very different deadlines.

I tend to work backwards in months. For example, if I want to promote my major event that takes place in mid-September, I want to be in the September issues of the monthly press, which are published at the end of August but have deadlines in early July, so my 'upside-down' timeline might look like this:

- Event: 15 September
- Local coverage appears in week running up to event
- Pitch detailed story to local radio and TV stations: 7 September
- Pitch detailed story to local newspapers: 1 September
- Write press release for local press with newly announced detail: last week in August
- Monthly magazine coverage appears: last week in August
- Event announcement covered: early August
- General release announcement of event to local press sent: late July
- Release announcing event to local weekly and broadcast press written: mid-July
- Release announcing event to monthly press sent: early July
- Press release for monthly local magazines written: late June
- Gathering information about event, images to support story, gathering local press contacts: throughout June.

A visual representation of this timeline can be seen on the next page.

Figure 2 PR campaign timeline

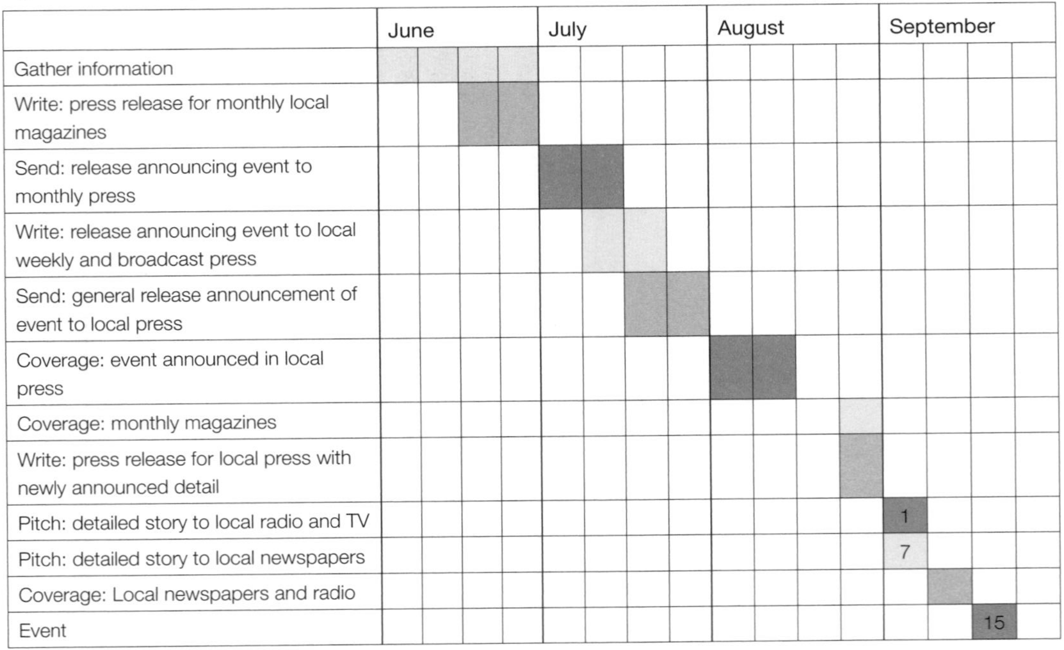

Event	June	July	August	September
Gather information				
Write: press release for monthly local magazines				
Send: release announcing event to monthly press				
Write: release announcing event to local weekly and broadcast press				
Send: general release announcement of event to local press				
Coverage: event announced in local press				
Coverage: monthly magazines				
Write: press release for local press with newly announced detail				
Pitch: detailed story to local radio and TV				1
Pitch: detailed story to local newspapers				7
Coverage: Local newspapers and radio				
Event				15

As you can see, this is a programme that needs to start three and a half months in advance, when I may well have another story or client that I'm promoting, so it needs some careful planning to ensure opportunities don't get missed. I find a spreadsheet or Gantt chart can really help with this type of 'backward' planning.

A lot of businesses struggle to get into monthly publications in particular, because they miss the publications' much earlier deadlines. This is a shame as monthly publications have a much longer shelf life than weeklies.

When you've written your PR strategy, don't let it reside on a hard drive somewhere, never looked at or referred to again. Like any business strategy document it needs to be an active document, regularly revisited, appraised and refreshed.

Position yourself as an expert for the broadcast media: start by listening to speech radio and list three programmes that you think you would be welcome on – ones that would cover your expertise. Then get in touch with the producer/ researcher when a story lands that you could comment on. Expect to be ignored. Rinse and repeat. Expect to get a call out of the blue when you least expect it.

Penny Haslam
journalist

Maintain your PR momentum

If you've followed the process and tips laid out in this book in roughly the order suggested, you should now be seeing some PR success. Hopefully you've written and sent a press release and been in touch with some of the key journalists on your target publications. Maybe you've already seen some results and secured media coverage, or you know it's coming soon.

PR isn't always a quick win, however. It takes time to build relationships with journalists. It can take a while to understand what makes a story newsworthy and to get a feel for the types of story that will excite a journalist. Your first attempts may not hit home, possibly because the story wasn't right for the media outlet or you just missed the deadline. It can also take several months for your press release to turn into coverage, especially if you're targeting monthly titles.

PR should be seen as a long-term game. Don't be downhearted if your first story disappears into the ether. Consider why it may not have worked. Wrong story pitched to the right publication – or vice versa? As a journalist starts to hear from and about you regularly, whether through a press release, social media or at industry events, they'll become more likely to give your stories some attention and to trust that you're going to send them ideas worth considering.

Once you do start getting coverage, PR has a tendency to snowball. One piece of coverage means that when you next send out a release other journalists are more likely to recognise you. As you become a trusted source of good stories and help, a journalist may come to you, asking you to take part in other stories or if you've got any ideas on a certain topic. More coverage means a higher profile and better reputation, meaning that more people want to write about you, as you're clearly a business of note. The first time a journalist (who you've always had to chase in the past) calls *you*, you know your PR campaign is starting to pay dividends.

When your PR campaign gets really successful, you may need to look at bringing in an in-house person to run the campaign or hire an external PR consultant or agency. While this can seem like a huge expense, a good PR professional really will be able to scale your PR campaign even further, with a fresh injection of ideas and new contacts.

I'm a firm believer, however, that every business should undertake their own PR, at least initially and quite possibly all the time. No one knows your business better than you. No one will enthuse about it, sell it and show their commitment to it more than you. No one has passion for it like you. That passion, knowledge and enthusiasm is what will sell your stories, your news and your business to the media.

I wish you the best of luck with your PR campaign, and I look forward to reading, watching and hearing all about your business in the media.

Reading list

Here are a few books and resources you might find useful as you develop your PR campaign.

Stevens, A. (2005) *The Pocket Media Coach*. How To Books.

A great resource for those undertaking media interviews.

Clapperton, G. (2013) *Hacked about: How to make press interviews and presentations productive for business*. Sunmakers.

Another excellent book on giving interviews, with a focus on business.

Rogers, D. (2015) *Campaigns that Shook the World: The evolution of public relations*. Kogan Page.

Fascinating book about some of the most effective and highest profile PR campaigns of the last 40 years that extrapolates lessons we can all learn but also traces the development of PR as a business discipline.

Blog: Ragan's PR Daily (prdaily.com)

Great blog that not only offers up case studies and 'how to's' but also offers tools, templates and ideas on running your PR campaign.